Would You Rather?

Witty Jacob

Would you rather go skydiving or go bungee jumping?

Would you rather not celebrate Christmas or not celebrate Easter?

Would you rather be the same age from now on and stay a kid or be reborn as a baby of the opposite gender and live normally?

Would you rather wear orange until the rest of your life or always wear green?

Would you rather have one best friend for the rest of your life or have 10 different best friends every four years?

Would you rather go to school with your legs tied all day or with your hands tied all day?

Would you rather meet and have dinner with your favorite singer or your favorite actor/actress?

Would you rather sing in front of the whole school or make a youtube video about your birthday party?

Would you rather lose the ability to lie or lose the ability to say no?

Would you rather go to a dance with your friends or go to a cinema with your parents?

Would you rather be an astronaut when you grow up or a doctor?

Would you rather only eat vegetables or have to eat whatever you want but only once a day?

Would you rather talk on the phone for 3 hours with your friends or go to play outside for 2 hours?

Would you rather have a hamster for a pet or a guinea pig for a pet?

Would you rather be a director of a movie or an actor/actress in a movie?

Would you rather feel angry all the time or sad all the time?

Would you rather only eat junk food or only eat sweets?

Would you rather be an influencer or a doctor?

Would you rather dream with no sound but in color or dream with sound but black and white?

Would you rather be really smart but ugly or not be very smart but beautiful?

Would you rather be great at school or be great at sports?

Would you rather play volleyball or play basketball?

Would you rather eat chips for the rest of your life or eat only ice cream for the rest of your life?

Would you rather live by the seaside or live in the mountains?

Would you rather sit all day for one day or only stand all day for one day?

Would you rather be a guest on Dancing With the Stars or on X-Factor?

Would you rather go on a cruiser for 3 months or go to live by the beach for 2 months?

Would you rather smell like food all the time or smell like a dog all the time?

Would you rather go camping in the woods with your friends or go to a fancy hotel with a pool and jacuzzi with your parents?

Would you rather make a Tik Tok video or a Youtube video?

Would you rather have 2 dogs as pets or have 5 cats as pets?

Would you rather be a politician or lawyer?

Would you rather go to a sleepover or have friends sleep at your house?

Would you rather live in a country that is sunny all the time or snowy all the time?

Would you rather sleep for 6 hours and not go to school or sleep how much you want and go to school?

Would you rather talk all the time or be quiet all the time?

Would you rather go to Disneyland and be there one day or go to the cinema ten times in a row?

Would you rather only eat salty things or only eat sweet things?

Would you rather only get presents for Christmas or only for your birthday?

Would you rather go to your grandmom and granddad for three days or go on a day trip to a zoo with school?

Would you rather be stranded on an island only with a knife or only with matches?

Would you rather see Narnia or go to Hogwarts?

Would you rather have a nice bear at home or a wild cheetah at home?

Would you rather have a new phone for a birthday or get a hiking trip with your friends and parents?

Would you rather have a pet snake or have a pet lizard?

Would you rather eat popcorn for breakfast or eat chips for dinner every night?

Would you rather be a major or be the president?

Would you rather live alone in a mansion or live in your home with your parents?

Would you rather prank call your dad or your mom?

Would you rather lose the ability to speak or lose the ability to hear?

Would you rather have three Christmases a year or two Birthdays a year?

Would you rather wear glasses or have braces?

Would you rather go skiing or go to the seaside?

Would you rather be blind or deaf?

Would you rather work as a zookeeper or work in an amusement park?

Would you rather find a lost pirate ship or find treasure in the jungle?

Would you rather meet Ariana Grande or meet Harry Styles?

Would you rather have a pet lion or a pet monkey?

Would you rather be rich and sad or poor and happy?

Would you rather live in a city or live in the suburbs?

Would you rather get three small presents or one big present for your birthday?

Would you rather eat snails or eat the hottest sauce on the world?

Would you rather live all alone in the city or with your best friends in the village?

Would you rather only have your laptop or only your telephone?

Would you rather fell into a well with water or fall into an empty pool filled with trash?

Would you rather drink lunch as a shake or drink a shake made out of spinach and kale?

Would you rather watch
Star Wars three times in
a row or eat the same
lunch three times
in a row?

Would you rather have
a rock band or
a pop band?

Would you rather be
Harry Potter or
Draco Malfoy?

Would you rather play
video games all day or
watch movies all day?

Would you rather be
Luke Skywalker or
Darth Vader?

Would you rather
sing really good or be
extraordinary at math?

Would you rather eat only breakfast or only eat dinner?

Would you rather have a dog or a cat?

Would you rather go to school dressed as a princess or dressed as Barbie?

Would you rather have only 5 classes in school but you don't like them or have 8 classes in school but you love them all?

Would you rather have a really cool park next to your house or a swimming pool next to your house?

Would you rather be super smart or super funny?

Would you rather only eat meat or only eat vegetables?

Would you rather be an amazing painter or be a pilot?

Would you rather have
a wolf or have
a jaguar?

Would you rather have a
house covered with candy
or have an underground
house?

Would you rather eat fish for a week or only eat potatoes for a week?

If you had two brothers, would you rather fight with your older brother or your younger brother?

Would you rather
go to Antarctica
or Madagascar?

Would you rather stay
awake by night and sleep
by day or stay awake by
day and sleep at night?

Would you rather have a baby brother or baby sister?

Would you rather live in a mansion on a hill or at a small house on the beach?

Would you rather have curly hair or straight hair?

Would you rather play with five kittens or play with five puppies?

Would you rather write a famous book or a famous song?

Would you rather have a broken arm or a broken leg?

Would you rather have blue short hair or green long hair?

Would you rather have one big house or two small ones?

Would you rather eat
fish or shellfish?

Would you rather
tell your crush you
like them or have
your friends tell
them?

Would you rather have
a custom made bicycle or
a custom made skateboard?

Would you rather play
football or be a football
coach?

Would you rather be in a school band or a school theatre group?

Would you rather own an island or a pirate ship?

Would you rather win a beauty contest or win a science competition?

Would you rather be able to have the ability to breathe under the water or the ability to swim really fast?

Would you rather write a book about your life or write a book about zombies?

Would you rather drink only water for the rest of your life or only eat vegetables and meat for the rest of your life?

Would you rather have purple hair or orange hair for one year?

Would you rather tell the truth, even if you know you will get into trouble or would you lie so you won't get into trouble?

Would you rather
do yoga or do pilates?

Would you rather live in a
van at the seaside or live in
a large apartment in the city?

Would you rather live
in China or Africa?

Would you rather drive
a motorcycle or a car?

Would you rather prank your crush or your best friend?

Would you rather be a ninja or a samurai?

Would you rather talk in public in front of five hundred people or sing in front of two hundred people?

Would you rather be a model or a professional dancer?

Would you rather sing all the time or dance all the time?

Would you rather have long hair or have short hair?

Would you rather be a zombie or kill a zombie?

Would you rather eat cereal with milk or with yogurt?

Would you rather eat kebabs for dinner or have cake for dinner?

Would you rather be able to turn into a werewolf or a vampire?

Would you rather be able to read minds or be able to teleport?

Would you rather fly or stop time?

Would you rather be your local superhero or be a famous wizard?

Would you rather work in a laboratory researching viruses or be an archeologist?

Would you rather call
your mom or your dad
if you fell into trouble?

Would you rather swim
very fast or run very fast?

Would you rather be a cheetah living in Africa or be a lion kept at home ?

Would you rather fart all day or have hiccups all day?

Would you rather have good but stupid humor or bad but smart humor?

Would you rather drink tea in the morning and eat what you want or drink soda in the morning but only eat vegetables?

Would you rather be
able to do a handstand
or to do a flip?

Would you rather be
famous and sad or
unfamous but happy?

Would you rather be able to go to the future or able to go to the past?

Would you rather watch a sci-fi movie or an animated movie?

Would you rather have an iPhone or Samsung?

Would you rather ski or snowboard?

Would you rather have
an older sister or a
younger brother?

Would you rather
have a car or a van?

Would you rather wear only pink clothes in school or only yellow clothes?

Would you rather smile all the time or be serious all the time?

Would you rather have a black cat or a white cat?

Would you rather fight with lightsabers or fight with swords?

Would you rather go to a concert or go to a water park?

Would you rather have a son or daughter when you grow up?

Would you rather lie to friends so they don't get hurt or would you tell them the truth even if it hurts them?

Would you rather have snails as a pet or have cockroaches as a pet?

Would you rather start
a new holiday or invent
a new sport?

Would you rather be
a superhero or a villain?

Would you rather be the funniest person in school or be the most beautiful person at school?

Would you rather be responsible for five cats or one baby?

Would you rather
work as a receptionist
or work as a nurse?

Would you rather go
to a circus or go to
a basketball game?

Would you rather go to the space station or go to Mars?

Would you rather have broken your arm on a skateboard or broke your legs while dancing?

Would you rather be
a vegan or a vegetarian?

Would you rather slow
dance to a fast song or
dance fast on a slow song?

Would you rather
listen to pop music
or rap music?

Would you rather be
able to do a handstand
or to do a flip?

Would you rather have a laptop or a personal computer?

Would you rather be fat and smart or thin and stupid?

Would you rather workout really hard only two times a week or workout only 30 minutes five times a week?

Would you rather go to school onlyfor three days a week, but the school would have 10 classes a day or go to school 5 times a week but have only 6 classes a day?

Would you rather have to clean the kitchen and your bedroom or only have to clean the toilet?

Would you rather be little sick four times a year or be really sick once a year?

Would you rather be
a computer engineer or a
video game programmer?

Would you rather have
only one leg and be
very rich or have both
legs and be poor?

Would you rather get an Olympic medal or an Oscar?

Would you rather shower only once a week or wear the same clothes for a week?

Would you rather own
an island or own a lake?

Would you rather sit in the
first row in school or sit in
the last row in school?

Would you rather smell like roses or smell like bubble gum?

Would you rather have your room painted black orpainted pink?

Would you rather get a three-hour massage or go to the spa?

Would you rather tell a joke just to make someone feel better or make them a card so they feel better?

Would you rather jump off a tree of a jump from the first floor of school?

Would you rather have a garden and have your own food or have to go to the store every day?

Would you rather play board games with your friends or play video games with your friends?

Would you rather breathe underwater or see underwater?

Would you rather play drums or play bass in a band?

Would you rather eat duck or chicken?

Would you rather
ski on water or
ski on snow?

If you had to, would you
rather rob a bank or
rob a jewelry?

Would you rather have your mom sing to you a lullaby every night before sleep or read a story before sleep?

Would you rather buy a bigger Christmas present for your mom or your dad?

Would you rather only eat potatoes or only eat meat?

Would you rather donate all of your money to your school or donate your money to your local animal shelter?

Would you rather stay late and be tired all day or go to sleep early and not be tired at all?

Would you rather go into space and live on another planet or live on go to space and come back to the earth?

Would you rather lost your phone or lost your wallet?

Would you rather have no toilet at home or have no kitchen at home?

Would you rather share food with your siblings or keep it all for yourself?

Would you rather write a personal journal or have a vlog about your life?

Would you rather have
a talking show or have
a cooking show?

Would you rather go
to the jungle or go to
a dessert?

Would you rather make a spaceship or be an inventor of the new phone?

Would you rather start a new television show or start a word wide science project?

Would you rather workout
for two hours or go for
a one-hour run?

Would you rather have
a duck as a pet or have
a chicken for a pet?

Printed in Great Britain
by Amazon